HOKUSAI

MASTERWORKS OF UKIYO-E

HOKUSAI
"THE THIRTY-SIX VIEWS OF MT. FUJI"

by Muneshige Narazaki

English adaptation by John Bester

KODANSHA INTERNATIONAL LTD.
Tokyo, New York & San Francisco

Distributors:

UNITED STATES: Harper & Row, Publishers, Inc., 10 East 53rd Street, New York, New York 10022. SOUTH AMERICA: Harper & Row, International Department. CANADA: Fitzhenry & Whiteside Limited, 150 Lesmill Road, Don Mills, Ontario. MEXICO & CENTRAL AMERICA: HARLA S. A. de C. V., Apartado 30–546, Mexico 4, D. F. BRITISH COMMONWEALTH (excluding Canada & the Far East): TABS, 7 Maiden Lane, London WC2. EUROPE: Boxerbooks Inc., Limmatstrasse 111, 8031 Zurich. AUSTRALIA & NEW ZEALAND: Book Wise (Australia) Pty. Ltd., 104–8 Sussex Street, Sydney. THAILAND: Central Department Store Ltd., 306 Silom Road, Bangkok. HONG KONG & SINGAPORE: Books for Asia Ltd., 30 Tat Chee Avenue, Kowloon; 65 Cresscent Road, Singapore 15. THE FAR EAST: Japan Publications Trading Company, P.O. Box 5030, Tokyo International, Tokyo.

Published by Kodansha International Ltd., 2–12–21 Otowa, Bunkyo-ku, Tokyo 112 and Kodansha International/USA, Ltd., 10 East 53rd Street, New York, New York 10022 and 44 Montgomery Street, San Francisco, California 94104. Copyright © 1968 by Kodansha International Ltd. All rights reserved. Printed in Japan.

LCC 68–17460
ISBN 0–87011–058–6
JBC 0371–780571–2361

First edition, 1968
Fifth printing, 1976

Contents

Adaptor's Preface

THE READER unfamiliar with modern Japan may wonder, as he turns these pages, what has become of Mt. Fuji in one of the world's greatest industrial nations. A word of reassurance: the mountain still stands unchanged. Japanese big business, though nothing if not enterprising, has so far found it neither desirable nor feasible to move it, alter its shape, or even install escalators. It is true that buses, replacing the horses of yesteryear, will take one as high as the fifth station—roughly where the vegetation stops—but the rest of the way one still scrambles up the ashes of the incomparable slag heap on foot. Even the summit, though crowded in the season, is so far garnished with little more than the inevitable huts and a meteorological station. Not a pinball parlor in sight.

To Tokyo, wrapping itself ever tighter in its shroud of smog, Mt. Fuji is increasingly a stranger. Those tourist photographs in which the mountain appears as a vast snowy form threatening to engulf the National Diet building, or to batter in your hotel window, use telescopic lenses with a degree of artistic license that would have shocked Hokusai. The observed reality, even when the smog permits, is smaller, more distant, and elusive.

This is not to say that this latter-day Edo does not offer some views of Mt. Fuji that would have interested Hokusai. In fact, one might easily make a tentative list for a new series of prints. That suburban train station platform, perhaps, with the familiar cone rising white and remote at the precise point where the parallel tracks are squeezed into infinity by the dusty-brown buildings crowding in on either side. . . . The river seen from the train at Tsurumi, where one's heart stirs with nostalgia for better and purer places at the sight of Mt. Fuji peering small and wistful over the factory-fringed horizon of Yokohama. . . . Or the hill at Akasaka where very occasionally, at dusk, I have seen it looming purple and angry against a blazing sunset that pales into their proper insignificance the neon signs on the jagged, black skyline below. . . . Surely the Hokusai who incorporated roofs, scaffoldings and timber yards into his compositions would make something of these, even while he pines for the integrity and homogeneity of the old scene?

Old Edo, after earthquake, war, and worse, has vanished forever. Outside the capital, a Hokusai reborn might begin to feel slightly more at home. The commuter who lives about an hour from Tokyo (on the coast, say, near Enoshima, where the Olympic yacht harbor has changed the shape of the island shown in the print) can at least recognize, as he gazes from the train window, that he is in Hokusai's country. Admittedly, the scene in the foreground is littered with houses and factories by now. But beyond them, he can see low hills that might have appeared in any of the "Thirty-six Views," while far beyond them again Mt. Fuji glides along silently after his train, peering slyly at him over the occasional dip in the hills.

Perhaps it would have been too much to hope that Hokusai's countryside would remain unchanged in an area that embraces the world's largest city and the stretch of coastal plain on which much of the nation's industry stands. Farther afield—but now not so very far from Tokyo—a great deal has in fact survived. The very intractability of Japan's terrain has helped here; in some areas there is little one can do except build roads. Thanks to the roads, one can now travel in comfort to various selected vantage points and enjoy views of Mt. Fuji and its surroundings as beautiful as anything Hokusai ever knew. One enjoys them, moreover, with the added security given by awareness of a parked car, a roadside restaurant, and a pay toilet with hot and cold running water immediately at one's right hand.

There are still blessings to be counted, then. But the large public that in Hokusai's day was showing such a keen interest in travel and in novelty for its own sake is still larger today, and its longing to see new places is less easily satisfied by looking at prints. It is more leisured and affluent, and there are more people ready to cash in on its tastes. To such people, Mt. Fuji and its environs are an obvious gold mine; the result, of course, is more hotels, more buses, more cable cars, more of everything.

Will good sense prevail before the beauty of the area is buried beneath a litter of "facilities" for the sightseer? It is a race against time. One almost wishes at times that, should things get too bad, the mountain would take things into its own hands: that the dormant volcano would rouse itself and purge the land about it of its impurities. After all, it was as recently as 1707 that Mt. Fuji last erupted; and a slumber of two and a half centuries is the merest catnap on the time scale of the geologist.

J. B.

Hokusai

HOKUSAI (1760–1849) is a type of figure who seems to recur again and again among great artists of all times and places: a compound of enormous vitality, longevity, impatience with the demands of conventional society, and eager questing after new styles to convey that something within the individual that clamors for expression. Considering the length of his life, we know little enough about him. Yet compared with, say, his great contemporary, Sharaku, he is well documented. We have a large body of work more or less accurately dated, a considerable number of his own writings, many contemporary references, and a mass of anecdote which, however suspect, by its very existence tells us something of the man.

If Hokusai as a human phenomenon reminds us of certain figures in the art history of other countries, there is also something familiar about the age in which he lived. From time to time, it seems, something ordains that in a certain country a certain art form shall enjoy a golden age—that there shall emerge in a short space of time, not one but many geniuses or near-geniuses who bring it to a perfection never known before and never after surpassed. The Japanese print in the latter half of the eighteenth century and the early nineteenth century enjoyed just such an extraordinary flowering.

Hokusai's life spanned almost the whole of that golden age. His art progressed in gradual stages from imitation of others to mature independence and the development of new forms, then went on to new heights while the form itself was lapsing into decadence, and finally survived to see itself become old-fashioned in its turn, and to be superseded.

Like most of those who created the art of the merchant class—as opposed to the "official" art of the shogunate and the high-ranking samurai—in eighteenth-century Edo, Hokusai lived most of his days in what was then the bustling business center of the city on the Sumida River. He was born in the ninth month of 1760 in Honjo, in the district of Edo known as Katsushika. The same area of modern Tokyo today is known as Katsushika Ward, and Katsushika was the surname which

Hokusai was to use in later life. His father's name was Kawamura, and in his childhood he used the given name of Tokitarō.

At the age of three, he was adopted by one Nakajima Ise, official polisher of mirrors to the shogunate. The intention was obviously that he should follow in his adoptive father's profession, but this was not to be. It is related that at the age of five he was already showing an interest in art and a fondness for sketching. At the age of nine, his name was changed to Tetsuzō, and one tradition has it that around this time—presumably because he showed no inclination to become a polisher of mirrors—he left his home and went to work for a lending library. Whether this story is true or not, it is a fact that he continued to use the name of his adoptive family, Nakajima, as his official name all through the rest of his life.

In his mid-teens, he was apparently apprenticed to a printer in Honjo Yokozunachō, where he learned the techniques of carving letters and pictures. This knowledge was to stand him in good stead in later years. Different artists differed greatly in the type of line they used, and it was the engraver's task to transfer the individual feeling of the original onto the block. One can imagine how the subtle interplay that occurred between the techniques of artist and engraver would have fascinated the young Hokusai, with his obsession with art.

During those same years, there was a great vogue for color prints, and the work of artists such as Suzuki Harunobu, Ippitsusai Bunchō, and Katsukawa Shunshō was in great demand among the general public. It was this, doubtless, that first fired Hokusai with the ambition to become a woodcut artist himself. Of all the artists whose work he came across, it seems to have been Shunshō, with his vivid, vigorous use of line, who made the deepest impression on him. It may be that in the course of running errands for the printer for whom he worked he attracted the attention of the great master, for at the age of eighteen he officially became his pupil. Very soon, he was a favorite of Shunshō's, and the following year he was given the artistic pseudonym of Shunrō, taking—as was common practice—one of the characters of his master's name in his own.

In the ten years from the time when he became a pupil of Shunshō—from 1778 until around 1788—Hokusai tried his hand at almost everything. He produced prints of famous beauties, of actors, of sumo wrestlers, and of birds and flowers. He also did landscapes in which he experimented with the Western-style perspective then in vogue. These latter works, though interesting, show neither the mastery of Western-style techniques nor the skill with landscapes that was to be apparent in his later works. From around the age of twenty, he also did illustrations for the popular novelettes that were enjoying such a vogue around this time. As an illustrator, he soon established a distinctive style of his own, and even tried his hand at writing the text of these novelettes himself.

In the very scope and variety of his work, however, there lay a source of trouble for the rising young artist. In order to understand this, it is necessary to know a little about the organization of ukiyo-e circles at the time. Originally, the world of ukiyo-e had (unlike the "official" art of traditional schools such as the Kanō and the Tosa) been a loosely organized group of artists. The only exception to this rule at first had been the Torii school, which had dominated the production of theatrical posters and the like; since the end of the seventeenth century, when it had first begun to specialize in such work, this school had maintained a strict family monopoly which admitted no interlopers. Now, in the eighteenth century, other ukiyo-e artists also began to feel the need for some such organization. The increasing wealth of the Edo merchant gave him increasingly extravagant tastes, and the polychrome print evolved partly in response to his new requirements. The possibilities of this new medium in turn encouraged the emergence of a succession of great artists who poured their genius into it. As they did so, a flourishing print publishing business gradually established itself, and this, together with the demand for large quantities of the more popular types of prints, led artists to form schools of followers who would carry on the styles which they had established and which had proved so lucrative. These followers in their turn often made special contracts with publishers under which they would provide, for example, illustrations to literary works such as popular novelettes.

A natural result was the development of exclusive artistic cliques aimed at protecting the interests of the artist and his followers in society. The very nature of such schools represented a restraint which a man of Hokusai's individuality was likely to find irksome. Moreover, around the time when Hokusai was first feeling his way into the various artistic forms then open to him, the Katsukawa school to which he belonged was facing a serious crisis. The ukiyo-e was just entering upon its golden age, and the world of prints was blessed with many fine artists, men such as Kiyonaga, Kiyomitsu, Bunchō, Shigemasa, Eishi, Utamaro, and Toyokuni. At such a time—when the Katsukawa school needed, above all, firm and imaginative leadership if it was to compete with such men for the public favor—its head, Shunshō, developed a preference for painting as opposed to the print, and began to accept commissions from wealthy houses. This took him increasingly into loftier social circles and away from the down-to-earth, highly competitive world of the ukiyo-e, and though he was much honored in name his practical influence declined greatly. His older followers, men such as Shun'ei and Shunkō, were too preoccupied with the slavish imitation of their master's style that was considered imperative in traditional artistic schools to produce any original work such as might get the school out of the doldrums.

Such a state of affairs must have caused considerable dissatisfaction among the more enterprising members of the school, and to no one more than a man of energy and teeming originality such as Hokusai. Nor, on their side, could the more conventionally minded members of the school have looked with much favor on a man who refused to let himself be restricted by the school's tradition. Although his style derived partly from the new type of portrait evolved by Shunshō, Hokusai also adopted elements from other styles, such as those of Shigemasa and Kiyonaga. This could only have been a source of annoyance to Shunkō and Shun'ei.

Even during his master's lifetime, Hokusai took advantage of Shunshō's comparative indifference to his pupils in order to behave with great artistic freedom. Quite apart from the requirements of his artistic conscience, such behavior was, from a realistic point of view, only wise. The ukiyo-e artist had to make his living in a practical world of hardheaded merchants and artisans, and there was no hope of making a real name himself so long as he turned out mere copies of his predecessors' work. This was true of the school as a whole, in fact, and when Shunshō died in 1792, it was soon to find that reflected glory was hardly enough to keep it going in an age of great individual masters.

Following the death of Shunshō, Hokusai seems to have followed his own bent with increasing freedom. He was friendly with an artist called Tsutsumi Tōrin (III), who claimed to derive his style from that of the great painter Sesshū (1420–1506) and actually signed his paintings "Sesshū XIII." With Tōrin, Hokusai did a number of joint works. Around the same time, he also studied the style of the Nampin school, which was popular for its pictures of birds and flowers drawn from nature. He dabbled in the techniques of the Literati style, and of Chinese, especially Ming painting. His interest in Western-style painting continued, too, though it was to take several more years before he acquired a true grasp of Western realistic techniques. He also learned the style of traditional Japanese painting (Yamato-e) under Sumiyoshi Hiroyuki of the Sumiyoshi school, though he seems not to have entered into any formal master-pupil relationship.

In the eyes of the scions of the Katsukawa school, such a man must have appeared as an unstable, mercurial being, and the way he moved from one style to another as downright arrogant. An incident that is said to have occurred around this time may well have been what put him finally beyond the pale. In 1794, shortly after Shunshō's death, Tōrin had arranged for Yūsen—son of the head of the Edo branch of the Kanō school, official painters to the Tokugawa shogunate—to instruct Hokusai in the style of that school. Therefore, when Yūsen was commanded by the shogunate, in that same year, to take his pupils and a number of professional painters to Nikkō to help in repairs of the Tokugawa mausoleum, it was quite natural for Hokusai to accompany them.

The group stopped on the way at an inn at Utsunomiya, and there, at the innkeeper's request, Yūsen did an impromptu picture of a child picking a persimmon off a tree. As Yūsen drew the scene, the child was standing on tiptoe, even though the bamboo pole he was holding projected above the persimmon branch. Hokusai commented to someone in private that Yūsen ought to have shown the child stretching up but still unable to reach the persimmon. His criticism reached the ears of Yūsen, who was furious; Hokusai was turned out and returned to Edo alone.

Whether or not such an incident served as the last straw, the fact is that, at the age of 34, Hokusai was expelled from the Katsukawa school. Whatever his personal feelings concerning the rival claims of a school's tradition and the artist's own artistic conscience, expulsion must have been a considerable blow to him in view of the increasing importance of such schools in dealing with publishers. The year was 1794—the very year, it is interesting to note, that the work of another great print artist, Sharaku, suddenly and apparently without any warning burst on the ukiyo-e scene in full maturity.

Hokusai was not long in finding his feet again. The very next year after his expulsion from the Katsukawa school, he acquired a new and comparatively distinguished position in artistic society as head of a school carrying on the traditions of the famous Kōrin school of decorative painting. The school had long been in abeyance, but in the mid-eighteenth century a pupil of Sumiyoshi Hiromori—father of the Hiroyuki with whom Hokusai studied—dubbed himself Tawaraya Sōri I (Tawaraya was the surname of Tawaraya Sōtatsu, one of the founders of the school) and thenceforth devoted his life to reviving its tradition. Sōri I had died fifteen years previously, and nobody had yet succeeded to his name. However, there was a young boy, Sōji, who at some time in the future was to take over the name and revive the tradition again. It was arranged that Hokusai should take Sōji as his pupil and in the meantime take the name of Sōri II for himself, so as to bring the illustrious name into use again.

With his originality and his energy, and with the added advantage that his new position gave him, Hokusai was set fair to becoming the leading figure of the ukiyo-e world. Other factors were in his favor too. In the second month of 1795, Sharaku produced his last series of prints and vanished from Edo, having flashed across its skies like a shooting star that soon burns itself out. The men who succeeded Sharaku in his field, men such as Kabukidō Enkyō and Utagawa Toyokuni, carried compromise with public demand too far. The public taste seems to have been deteriorating at this time, possibly on account of the demoralization occasioned by corruption in official administration and the bewildering new ideas that were abroad at the time. The Torii school of actor-prints, and still more the portraits of the Katsukawa school, were showing a pitiful decline. In 1796, moreover, Tsutaya Jūzaburō, the leading figure in the publishing world, died. Utamaro, whose reputation had been inseparably bound up with that of the house of Tsutaya, may have been affected by this, for his art—as seen in the series of what he pretentiously called "Utamaro-type beauties"—deteriorated into empty mannerism. The decline of Utamaro left a serious gap among artists producing prints of "famous beauties."

This gap was partly filled by Hokusai himself, who, as Sori II, started depicting a new type of "beauty," shown in scenes of great charm and romantic warmth. These prints, popularly known as "Sōri beauties," enjoyed a great vogue. At the same time, he was starting to produce prints for the *kyōka ehon*, small books in which pictures were matched to examples of the humorous and satirical verse popular at the time. His prints now placed an increased emphasis on the landscape element, and showed a strength of line and attention to detail that owed much to his studies of Chinese painting and gave a new virility to the rather effete ukiyo-e.

As head of the Sōri school, Hokusai also produced paintings which attempted to recreate and develop its tradition. One can well imagine, however, that Hokusai found himself no happier in trying to confine himself within this tradition than he had been as a member of the Katsukawa school. In the world of ukiyo-e, where his heart lay, slavish adherence to one's predecessor's style, together with the formalistic emphasis laid on a school's pedigree and the position of its head, were meaningless, particularly to a man like Hokusai, who favored the new rationalistic and realistic approach that was abroad at the time.

It was only four years after he had succeeded to the name of Sōri that Hokusai broke with the Tawaraya family. The official reason was that Sōji, who was in the true line of succession, had acquired sufficient proficiency to succeed to the leadership of the school. In late 1798, Hokusai returned the name to him, and set himself up as an independent artist.

The period of over thirty years that began in 1799, when Hokusai was in his thirty-ninth year, and ended with the completion of his great "Thirty-six Views of Mt. Fuji" saw the steady maturing of his art and the production of his most significant work. Although this work shows an almost bewildering profusion and variety, it is possible, perhaps, to sum it up under the following seven listings.

1. He inaugurated a new phase in the use of Western modes of expression. This is to be seen in his oil paintings and copperplates. In his "Ushigafuchi, Kudan," for example, his attempt to create a sense of space represents a creative use of Western techniques as opposed to the awkward imitations of Western perspective which enjoyed a temporary vogue as a kind of interesting optical illusion.

2. At the same time, he portrayed the manners and appearance of various parts of the city of Edo in a large number of works—pictures of famous beauties and genre scenes, and *kyōka ehon*—which emphasized the more characteristically Japanese lyrical qualities, thus raising the popular "illustrated guide" type of work to a new artistic level.

3. He applied his characteristic brilliance of technique to illustrations for *yomihon* and other literary works, producing works of a robustness and attention to detail that could confidently accompany the literary extravagances of, say, a writer of fantasies such as Bakin.

4. He produced brush paintings of women in various everyday scenes which had an extraordinary sensuous charm. They include a number of enduring

masterpieces such as the "Drunken Beauty" and "Gathering Shellfish at Low Tide."

5. From the time of his trip to the Osaka-Kyoto area in 1812, he began turning out volumes of a new type of sketch, in which he developed an astonishing mastery in portraying human figures, as well as albums of studies which had a great educative, as well as artistic value.

6. He completed his masterpiece, "The Thirty-six Views of Mt. Fuji," which he had started work on in 1823. To gather material for the series, he traveled through remote country districts, especially those around Mt. Fuji, exposing himself to the countryside in all its moods. As a result, he succeeded in opening up hitherto unknown realms in the depiction of nature and gave the world an imperishable masterpiece.

7. He demonstrated an extraordinary diversity and invention in landscape series and in large- and medium-sized prints of "bird-and-flower" themes.

In none of these works, not even in the pictures of beautiful women turned out to meet the popular demand, did Hokusai's eye fail him or his feeling give way to facile sentimentality. The sureness of his grasp of his subject is astonishing. For long years, Hokusai dominated the field of popular art virtually unchallenged—at least, wherever originality, dignity and taste were the criteria. Most of the artists who had belonged to the Katsukawa school had given up the ukiyo-e. The only two members of note who were left in the first decade of the nineteenth century were Shunkō, now feeble and decrepit, and Shun'ei, who was desperately flogging his failing powers in an effort to rival Hokusai.

The new darlings of the masses were the artists of the Utagawa school, Chōbunsai Eishi and his pupils, and the men of the Kikugawa school, though the Utagawa school and its ramifications were tending to monopolize the ukiyo-e at the expense of the others. Pandering to the popular passion for the theater, these men turned out an unending stream of pictures of the theater and individual actors, and also catered to the deteriorating taste of the early nineteenth century by producing a large number of prints of women in a frankly sensational and lascivious vein.

Hokusai's works obviously sold well, and one would not expect him to have been poor during this period. We know, in fact, that around 1808, when he was forty-eight, he had a stylish new studio built, and held a party to celebrate its completion at a fashionable restaurant, to which he invited a large number of artists and men of letters; a copy of the invitation to this party still survives. We know, too, that he had around twenty or thirty followers of his own at this same period, and even more at a later date. This suggests that he had a considerable standing in Edo society. Yet we also know as historical fact that he changed his dwelling on an extraordinary number of occasions—ninety-three times in all, according to popular tradition. Tradition also says that he was perennially poor and indifferent to worldly affairs—that when a publisher came to bring him his fees and found him hard at work, Hokusai would wave in the direction of the wastepaper basket and tell him to put the money in it; and that those who came to collect debts would have to delve in the same basket for their money.

It seems likely that he was a genuine example of that hackneyed type—the great artist who is truly indifferent to such matters, and who is able to accept great fluctuations in his material circumstances with equanimity, so long as he is absorbed in his work. This is borne out by a large number of other anecdotes concerning his individualistic—not to say eccentric—behavior. Many of them may well be apocryphal; yet their nature, and their very existence, surely testify to a personality that in its scale and intensity set him apart from his contemporaries.

In 1804—one such anecdote runs—at the ceremonies marking the regular unveiling to the public of the statue of Kannon at the Gokoku-ji temple at Otowa in Edo, Hokusai is said to have astonished the crowd by painting an enormous half-length picture of the Buddhist patriarch Bodhidharma on a composite piece of paper laid out by the side of the main hall. "A horse might pass through the mouth and a man take his ease on one of the eyes," declared one account, which also described the saké tubs full of ink, the brooms used for brushes, and the other materials needed to produce the work. On later occasions, he painted a huge picture of a horse, and another of the deity Hotei. In 1817, on his second trip to the Osaka-Kyoto area, he painted another enormous picture of Bodhidharma before an admiring throng. Yet the same man is said to have had an eye so sharp, and a technique so fine that he could draw two sparrows on a grain of rice.

It is also told that one year, when the shogun stopped at the Asakusa temple on his way falconing, he summoned the painter Tani Bunchō and—an extraordinary honor for an artist of the merchant class—Hokusai, and commanded them to produce works on the spot for his amusement. Hokusai's landlord, on receipt of preliminary warning of the command, was so overwhelmed that for seven or eight days before Hokusai was to appear before the shogun, he kept the strictest watch over him, not even allowing him to leave the house without good reason.

The day came and Hokusai, not in the least awed, entered the august presence carrying a basket. He stretched out a long roll of paper on the floor, drew a few dark-blue lines along it with a brush, then took a chicken from the basket. As those present watched with bated breath, he coated the chicken's feet with vermilion ink of the kind used for seals, and turned it loose on the paper. The chicken ran away over the paper, leaving a trail of brilliant footprints as it went.

Hokusai prostrated himself before the shogun. "Autumn Maple Leaves Drifting on the Tatsuta River," he announced, and with one more obeisance withdrew. Afterwards he complained that the constricting formality of the occasion had been a sore trial for him. The incident made Hokusai's name widely known; orders for pictures came in thick and fast, and many aspiring artists came to study with him.

Another anecdote tells how, during the period when Hokusai was taking his meals at the home of the novelist Bakin, the latter gave him some money, as he had none with which to pay for the service on the anniversary of his mother's death. One evening while visiting with Bakin, Hokusai happened to draw from his pocket the paper in which the money had been wrapped. He blew his nose in the paper, which was now empty, and threw it away.

"What have you done with the money?" demanded Bakin. Hokusai laughed. "I got myself a good meal and something to drink," he said. To spend money on offerings to the Buddha, hiring a priest, and having the scriptures read was nothing more than a meaningless show in Hokusai's mind. He felt it far more sensible to use the money himself. "Surely," he said, "the best way to show real filial piety is to make sure one lives to a good old age oneself."

Hokusai also changed his artistic pseudonym frequently, passing his previous name on to one or another of his followers. He changed his name thus some thirty times, and if one examines the list of names in relation to the works on which he was engaged at the time, it seems probable that a change of name indicated some change in his style. As likely as not, his passion for moving to new quarters was also bound up with a restless artistic spirit that was always looking for a new environment to match his mood.

"The Thirty-six Views of Mt. Fuji" seems to have marked the high-water line of his art. He was in his early seventies at the time. He was to live another decade and a half yet, and to produce a large mass of work, much of it far from inconsiderable. For example, it was probably after the completion of the "Thirty-six Views" that he did works such as *Shokoku Meikyō Kiran* ("Unusual Views of Famous Bridges Throughout the Country"), *Shokoku Takimawari* ("Waterfalls Throughout the Country"), and *Ryūkyū Hakkei* ("Scenes from the Ryukyus"), which show a remarkable diversity and invention in depicting landscapes. Nevertheless, he never reached quite the same heights again.

Part of the cause may have lain, of course, in old age and failing powers. One cannot help suspecting, though, that it was due partly to a creeping lack of self-confidence in the face of waning public interest in his work. Hokusai's own writings suggest that he was humble before his art and ever eager to find ways to improve it; yet they also suggest that in his heart of hearts he was not so humble before his public's powers of judgment. It must have been a great shock for such a man to find himself gradually supplanted in the limelight by a younger and—he doubtless considered—inferior artist.

It is remarkable that the common people of Edo should have been the patrons of a body of art which can rank among the finest in the nation's history. Yet the public was, when all is said and done, less interested in abiding artistic values than in novelty. The ukiyo-e as a whole had declined sadly since its heyday, and Hokusai, great though he was, was in a sense a lone figure fighting a rising tide of vulgarity. Even so, the form was to produce one last master who, though his work shows traces of the facility, vulgarity and sentimentality characteristic of decadence, was nevertheless, at his best, an individual and great artist. Hiroshige had been born when Hokusai was already a mature man of thirty-seven. His landscape prints had for many years been enjoying an increasing popularity, and finally in 1833, not long after the completion of Hokusai's "Thirty-six Views of Mt. Fuji," he produced his celebrated "Fifty-three Stations on the Tōkaidō." At once it became the rage of the town—almost as though Hokusai's series had never been published.

As though in an attempt to challenge the younger man's popularity, Hokusai in 1834 published his *Hundred Views of Mt. Fuji,* not as a series of color prints but as three picture book volumes in black and white. They included some very fine work, even though the necessity for producing a hundred variations on the same theme strained even Hokusai's inventiveness. But they failed to restore him to his previous unchallenged position, and they proved in the event to have been almost a kind of artistic farewell. Thereafter, he spent much time turning out pictures of warriors and women, badgers and ghosts in a style which no one wanted any more, while a majority of his published works consisted of picture books, mostly on historical and literary themes which had an undoubted educational value but were fatally old-fashioned.

His will to improve his art persisted to the end. In a postscript to the *Hundred Views,* he declared that at seventy-four he had at last penetrated to the true nature of all things, and announced his intention of living to the age of one hundred and ten, boasting that his art would by then have become indistinguishable from life itself. Even at the age of eighty-eight, in a manual on painting called *Ehon Saishiki-tsū,* he was still declaring that he would live to be over a hundred. But his last years seem in fact to have been lived out in conditions of hardship. Of his family, only one daughter was left with him to look after him in his declining years. Most of his disciples seem to have died—or to have left him, which is not surprising if the tales of his irregular habits and eccentricity are true. At one stage in his last years he moved to Uraga, on the opposite side of the bay from Edo, and a letter survives which he wrote at this period to his publisher, asking for money. It has a picture of a mendicant priest bowing and begging for alms, and it complains that despite his great age he had not even enough clothes to keep him warm. Yet in the same letter he writes of his unflagging energy and his artistic ambitions for the future.

He returned to his beloved Edo before long, and lived to change his address several times more before he died on the eighteenth day of the fourth month of 1849. He was buried at the Seikyō-ji temple in Nagazumi-chō, Asakusa. Tradition has it that, on his deathbed, he asked for another ten years—or if not ten, five at least—so that he could become a real artist.

He died in straitened circumstances, and knew the double bitterness of the popular idol who has been supplanted by a younger rival. But history has been kinder to Hokusai than the public of Edo. It has shown that there is room enough in Japanese art for both a Hokusai and a Hiroshige.

Résumé of Hokusai's Life

(Hokusai's age at the time of each event noted is given in parentheses)

1760   Born in the ninth month of this year at Honjo Wari-gesui, Edo, in the general area known as Katsushika and now part of Katsushika Ward, Tokyo. Family name Kawamura, childhood given name Tokitarō. In later years adopts the name Katsushika as his own artistic surname.

1763 (3)   Around this time adopted by Nakajima Ise, polisher of mirrors to the Tokugawa shogunate.

1765 (5)   Said to have shown a fondness for pictures around this age. Suzuki Harunobu and others begin to publish polychrome prints.

1769 (9)   Around this time changes his given name to Tetsuzō. One tradition says that he leaves his adopted home, but all his life he continues to use "Nakajima" as his official surname.

1774 (14)   Studying the techniques of woodblock engraving around this time.

1775 (15)   Said to have done part of the engraving for the *sharebon* (illustrated novelette) *Rakujo Gōshi*.

1778 (18)   Becomes pupil of Katsukawa Shunshō.

1779 (19)   Takes the name Katsukawa Shunrō; prints of actors survive from this period.

1780 (20)   Does illustrations for popular novelettes, including many of the type known as *kibyōshi*.

1785 (25)   Around this time starts producing polychrome prints. Does interesting but not completely successful landscapes. Torii Kiyonaga is at the height of his popularity.

1792 (32)   His teacher Katsukawa Shunshō dies, and the Katsukawa school begins to disintegrate. The ukiyo-e enters on its golden age; masters such as Utamaro and Eishi publish large numbers of works.

1793 (33)   Around this period studies with Kanō Yūsen.

1794 (34)   Expelled from the Katsukawa school. Associates with the painter Tsutsumi Tōrin. Tōshūsai Sharaku begins his brief artistic career.

1795 (35) Takes the name of Tawaraya Sōri II.

1796 (36) Said to have studied with Sumiyoshi Hiroyuki around this period.

1797 (37) "Sōri-type" pictures of beautiful women enjoy a vogue. Hiroshige born.

1798 (38) In winter of this year returns the name Sōri to his pupil Sōji. Takes the name Hokusai as his chief artistic pseudonym.

1799 (39) Publishes *Azuma Asobi* with excellent illustrations in a style influenced by Chinese painting and showing scenes from life in Edo.

1800 (40) Develops a new style for single-sheet prints. Publishes the *kyōka ehon* (a book of pictures with humorous verse), *Tōto Meisho Ichiran* ("A Guide to Famous Sights in Edo").

1802 (42) Exploring new avenues in Western-style modes of expression. Publishes *Itako Zekku*, which is banned by the authorities.

1804 (44) Does an enormous picture of Bodhidharma at the Gokoku-ji temple in Edo. Publishes "Fifty-three Stations on the Tōkaidō," a series of prints. Several other series published around this time.

1806 (46) Around this time publishes the *kyōka ehon*, *Sumidagawa Ryōgan Ichiran* ("A Guide to Both Banks of the Sumida River").

1807 (47) Begins to concentrate on illustrations for *yomihon*, another type of popular novelette, creating an entirely new style of illustration.

1808 (48) Sets up an impressive new studio at Kamezawa-chō in Edo.

1810 (50) Said to have done posters for the Ichimura-za theater, without finding popular favor.

1811 (51) Polychrome prints begin to outnumber illustrations in his output. Paints a picture of Tametomo with an inscription by the well-known novelist Bakin.

1812 (52) Journeys to the Kansai area, stays at Nagoya. Publishes *Ryakuga Haya-shinan*, a manual on painting.

1814 (54) Publishes the first volume of the *Sketchbooks*. Production of manuals on painting increases.

1819 (59) Completes the first ten volumes of the *Sketchbooks*. Starts work on further volumes.

1823 (63) Said to have begun publication of "The Thirty-six Views of Mt. Fuji" around this time.

1831 (71) "Thirty-six Views" still being published around this time. The ukiyo-e landscape print makes great strides thanks to Hokusai and Hiroshige, who is increasingly active.

1833 (73) Around this period publishes *Ryūkyū Hakkei* and *Shokoku Takimawari*. Hiroshige springs into public favor with publication of his "Fifty-three Stations on the Tōkaidō."

1834 (74) Publishes the *Hundred Views of Mt. Fuji*. Also publishes *Shokoku Meikyō*

Kiran and a number of prints of birds and flowers. Around this time retires temporarily to Uraga in the country not far from Edo.

1835 (75) Publishes the *Hyakunin Isshu Uba ga Etoki*; 28 in the series survive, together with preliminary drawings for others.

1836 (76) Begins to concentrate on brush paintings.

1842 (82) Starts work on an album of paintings, *Nisshin Joma-chō*; completes it in the twelfth month of the following year.

1845 (85) Goes on a long trip to northwest Honshū.

1848 (88) Publishes *Ehon Saishiki-tsū*, a work on painting for the student. Publishes local survey drawings.

1849 (89) Dies on the eighteenth day of the fourth month, interred at the Sei-kyō-ji temple in Asakusa, Edo.

"The Thirty-six Views of Mt. Fuji"

The series of woodcut prints entitled "The Thirty-six Views of Mt. Fuji" is generally held to be Hokusai's masterpiece; quite possibly, it has been more widely acclaimed throughout the world, and had more influence on Western artists, than any other work of Japanese art. Publication of individual prints in the series is believed to have begun around 1823, and seems to have been completed around 1831. There are, in fact, forty-six prints in all, ten further prints having been added to the original series around 1831. Hokusai may have intended to continue the series still further, but he was already an old man, and he seems to have been discouraged by the popularity that a fickle public was according to Hiroshige's newly published series, "Scenes of Life in Edo" and "The Fifty-three Stations on the Tōkaidō."

There is no clue to the original order of publication within the series, though what appear to be the ten additional works are distinguished by the use of black lines instead of the dark-blue lines used in all the rest. Some prints obviously represent a greater artistic maturity than others, and—as is only to be expected in such an extensive work—there are comparative failures among them, but the collection as a whole maintains an extraordinarily high level, and includes a number of prints generally acknowledged as masterpieces. Even those works that have been comparatively neglected often repay close study by yielding up unexpected beauties.

With the exception of two or three works that deal exclusively with Mt. Fuji, all the prints show the mountain as seen from various points, some near, some far, in the neighboring provinces. In most prints, the exact spot is more or less identifiable from the title. In many cases, however, Hokusai used the actual view as the merest pretext for creating landscapes of his own in which, by including scenes of life in the country and the city of Edo, he also explored the relationship between man and his natural environment.

In its origins, the ukiyo-e was chiefly concerned in the portrayal of manners and customs, and this type of ukiyo-e had already enjoyed a long history. It was natural, thus, that even when it depicted natural scenery, it should also include human and social elements. In this, it was similar to the *Yamato-e* of ancient times, which had always shown human figures in its depictions of nature. The *Yamato-e,* however, declined before it could be touched by any new humanist outlook. It failed to evolve the consciousness of nature as distinct from man that is necessary if a true landscape painting is to emerge. The ukiyo-e, however, with its roots in a more plebeian soil, was to break the old bonds and achieve independence for the landscape in the modern sense. And the greatest step forward in this direction was taken in the work of Hokusai.

Like his predecessors in the world of the ukiyo-e, Hokusai originally specialized in the portrayal of human figures and human mores. The majority of his works are genre pictures, and a large proportion of the "Thirty-six Views" contain human figures somewhere in the prints. Yet the relationship between man and nature here is a new one. Even without the figures the prints could exist as landscapes in their own right, and finally, sometime in the latter part of the 1820's, Hokusai produced prints that abandoned the human element completely.

The development of the ukiyo-e landscape as seen in Hokusai's work, and in the work of Hiroshige, who supplanted him in his old age as darling of the print collector, was the product not only of these two artists' own genius, but of the intellectual background against which they worked. The arts of Edo—not only the print, but music, drama, and literature also—had long been, essentially, an embodiment of the energy of the merchant class in terms of its own, comparatively restricted everyday life. However, from around the year 1800 the intellectual life of this same merchant class began to broaden its horizons remarkably, and there developed a new interest in travel, in other parts of the country, and in nature, and a new sense of the unity of the nation and its culture. Its art became not so much the art of one restricted segment of society, as an art of the masses in the broad sense. This, together with the new interest in rationalistic and scientific ideas which even the Tokugawa regime could not stifle forever, served to create a new individualism and humanism (both these terms, of course are used here in the relative sense; they do not mean exactly what they would in the West today), and these in turn manifested themselves in subtle ways in the art of Hokusai and Hiroshige.

Even so, there were great differences between the work of the two men. Hiroshige's approach to nature was colored by the characteristically Japanese, emotive outlook of the nation's poetry. Hokusai completely rejected this national brand of sentimentality, and sought to apprehend nature in its more universal aspects— that is, in its physical reality and as a source of unending energy and continuous creation. He felt his own creativity as part of the process of creation that he saw going on all about him. His art was subjective insofar as he refashioned and reorganized nature to suit his own will; he also seems to identify the energy of nature with his own inner energy, so that, whether consciously or unconsciously, he makes his waves claw and clutch like human hands and his clouds writhe with an almost supernatural life. Yet his art was also objective in that, as we have already suggested, he recognized nature as a force outside man which each man experiences and recreates with his own senses and his own intellect. And, in doing this, he also recognized man himself in a way that is highly significant in the history of Japanese art and that may explain one aspect of his appeal in the West.

This new individualism, this sense of freedom to manipulate nature and to create ever new forms, obviously ties up with another feature of Hokusai's art that distinguished it from the "official" art of the time: the endless inventiveness—at times, the eccentricity—of his composition. One detects, of course, certain recurring features, notably the fondness, pointed out by many critics, for building up a picture from a combination of triangles and circles (or parts of circles). Yet whether he is showing Mt. Fuji in closeup to the exclusion of everything else, or whether it is only a distant and tiny point of focus in a larger scene, his "Thirty-six Views" are a virtuoso display of his skill in producing variations on a visual theme.

Nowhere is this virtuosity more apparent than in the famous "Great Wave Off Kanagawa" (Plate 4), one of the works that most astonished Western artists of the nineteenth century when Hokusai's work first swam into their ken. This particular print, in fact, sums up many of the most individual characteristics of the series as a whole. It is a good example of the "circle-and-triangle" composition. It bears eloquent witness to the almost demonic energy that possessed Hokusai and that he saw at work in nature all about him. It shows the effective use of simple color that was such a revelation to artists in the West. And it is an interesting case of the special relationship between the human element and nature that exists throughout "The Thirty-six Views of Mt. Fuji."

In its intrinsic interest, the human element in the prints parallels and rivals that of the landscape aspect. Almost all the "Thirty-six Views" contain human figures shown engaged in various activities. The prints are, in a sense, intensely theatrical: the figures are on a stage, as it were, and the natural scene is carefully stage-managed by the artist so as to provide a perfect setting for them. Yet it never becomes a simple background.

Nor, on the other hand, do the figures ever serve merely to provide a point of focus in the scene. Never, as in early *Yamato-e* landscapes, are they mere lifeless puppets incorporated as part of an overall effect. On the contrary, they have a magnificent,   believable life of their own that is as much a raison d'être for the works as the landscapes themselves.

One only needs to glance at the many volumes of Hokusai's *Sketchbooks* that preceded the "Thirty-six Views" to realize the intense interest he felt in the human body, whether at rest or in motion, and the extraordinary energy with which he studied it. As a result of long years of practice, he acquired a feeling for the movements of the human body, and for the emotional significance of particular postures or gestures, together with a remarkable ability to convey a sense of life, or a particular attitude or facial expression, with the utmost economy of line. Nowhere is this ability seen more clearly than when he depicts human figures moving in the distance (as in Plates 23 and 26, for example). The extreme smallness of the figures allows for no detail at all—yet even so, they are as full of life and motion as any of his larger figures.

The attitude Hokusai expresses towards his human figures is another characteristic that sets him apart from other artists of his day. In the "Thirty-six Views," the artist succeeds in identifying himself completely with the common people—not only with the merchants and artisans of the towns, but with the poor people of the country, living their lives out in the hills and fields far from the sophisticated comforts of the city. He shows them with humor, and with an entirely unsentimental sympathy that can be very moving. Above all, they are alive; even when a face is hidden beneath a large hat (as with the man nodding in the bows of the boat in Plate 28, or the small figure fishing in the river in Plate 55), one feels that Hokusai has portrayed a real human being with feelings and a life of his own.

It is remarkable how this human element is incorporated with the landscape surrounding it without either dominating or being dominated. It is as though Hokusai achieved a perfect fusion of two aspects of his art that had been developing parallel to each other—the interest in the human figure and in humanity as such, and the fresh interest in nature for its own sake that was in part a product of the intellectual atmosphere of his period.

There are a few works in the series, however, in which Hokusai seems to have felt impelled to go still further to achieve a new form of landscape art. In these works man disappears from the scene completely. This group, significantly enough, includes some of the most famous works of all. It would almost seem that Hokusai had achieved some identification with the natural world in which any suggestion of human society had become irrelevant. In the "Great Wave Off Kanagawa," already mentioned above, man has almost completely disappeared, but one's chief impression from this print is, rather, of the force of nature and man's impotence in the face of it. In "Thunderstorm Below the Mountain" (Plate 40), there is still strife and shadow in the world below, though the mountain's peak rises clear and untroubled above it. In the celebrated "Red Fuji," however, all is serenity and light. This extraordinary print—superficially one of the simplest in the series—has elicited more admiration and exerted more influence on Western artists than any of the others in the series. It displays some of the characteristics of Hokusai's work in their most basic form, and it is worthwhile in conclusion, perhaps, to examine in more detail the essence of its originality.

The first interesting thing is the composition, which, though not obviously eccentric as in some other prints in the series, is very characteristic of Hokusai's methods—and, ultimately, of the Japanese sensibility as such. Hokusai places the peak of the mountain at the top right of the picture, with seven-tenths of the mountain's visible width to the left, and only three-tenths to the right. On the left, there is a long, gentle slope with a great space of sky above it; on the right, the slope is cut off abruptly. One sees at work here the characteristic Japanese fondness for asymmetry. The type of rationalistic, formal symmetry to be seen in many Western gardens is not unknown in Japan, of course. This formal symmetry is evident in Buddhist temples and statues, where orderly right-left symmetry was associated with spirituality, and it also occurred in early palaces and aristocratic dwellings, where it was associated with rank and nobility. Yet throughout history this purely visual symmetry has not satisfied the Japanese sensibility. The "Red Fuji" is the most clear-cut example to be found in the series, but other instances can easily be found. In the "Red Fuji," balance is restored unconsciously in the viewer's mind, which supplies the remainder of the right-hand slope and the actuality of the unseen mountainside. This love of asymmetry can be found in many other forms of Japanese art through the ages. The unconscious sense of "something lacking," and the natural urge of the mind to relieve the tension thus created by supplying what is not there, is a vital element in the dynamics of Japanese art, and one of its chief means of creating aesthetic pleasure.

Secondly, the work demonstrates in its ultimate form the love of simplification and the ability to create a maximum of effect with a minimum of detail that is apparent in the other prints, too. All that is shown is the mountain and the sky above it, with its layers of fleecy white clouds moving in the gentle breeze. It is late summer. The snow which caps the mountain at other times has disappeared, save for a little still lying, unmelted, in the gullies that score the mountain's flanks. The time of day? It might be the moment when the rays of the setting sun are reflected red on Mt. Fuji's slopes, in a last blaze of glory before the mountain is transformed into a dark, mysterious silhouette. More probably, however, the print is a memory of Mt. Fuji at dawn, of that moment of silent exaltation when the sun, appearing over the horizon beyond the sea, illuminates the clouds in what, until a moment previously, was a darkened sky, and the whole peak flushes with the rosy glow of dawn. As with human beings, so with nature: Hokusai had a genius for capturing one brief, particular moment in time through the very simplest of means.

Finally, the "Red Fuji" sums up another aspect of Hokusai's art which must have astonished the first Western artists who came into contact with it—his use of color. Although there are subtle gradations of color when one looks closely at the work, and despite the large patch of green at the bottom, the print relies for its chief effect on the bold contrast of two colors, the red of the mountain's flanks and the deep azure of the sky (or three colors, if one counts the white of the clouds that hover in the sky beyond the mountain). Before Hokusai, it was an accepted artistic convention that Mt. Fuji was white, and so it was portrayed by artist after artist. Hokusai, however, defiantly showed it whatever color—red, blue, white, black—it appeared to him to be at the time. He rescued nature from prettifying, stultifying tradition and made it a matter for personal experience, something for the artist to interpret with his own sensibility. In this, he was both realistic and more than realistic. And in works such as the "Red Fuji," he was anticipating the use of color in the modern art of the West.

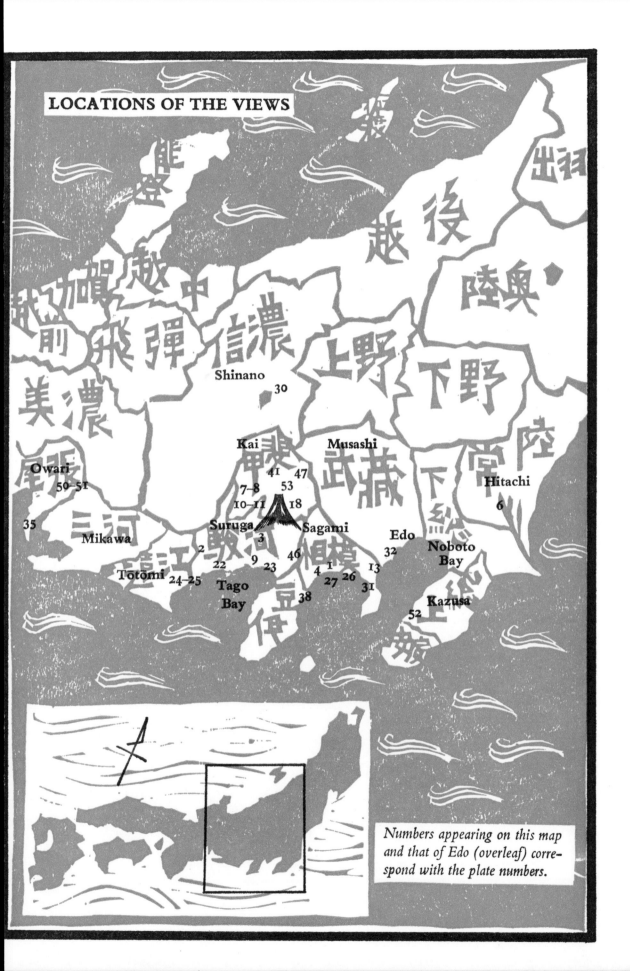

LOCATIONS OF THE VIEWS

Shinano
30

Kai

Owari
50–51

Musashi

41 47
7–8 53
10–11 18

Hitachi
6

35

Mikawa

Suruga 3

Sagami

Edo
32

Noboto
Bay

2

Totōmi

22
9 23

46

4 1

13

24–25
Tago
Bay

27 26

31

Kazusa

38

52

Numbers appearing on this map and that of Edo (overleaf) correspond with the plate numbers.

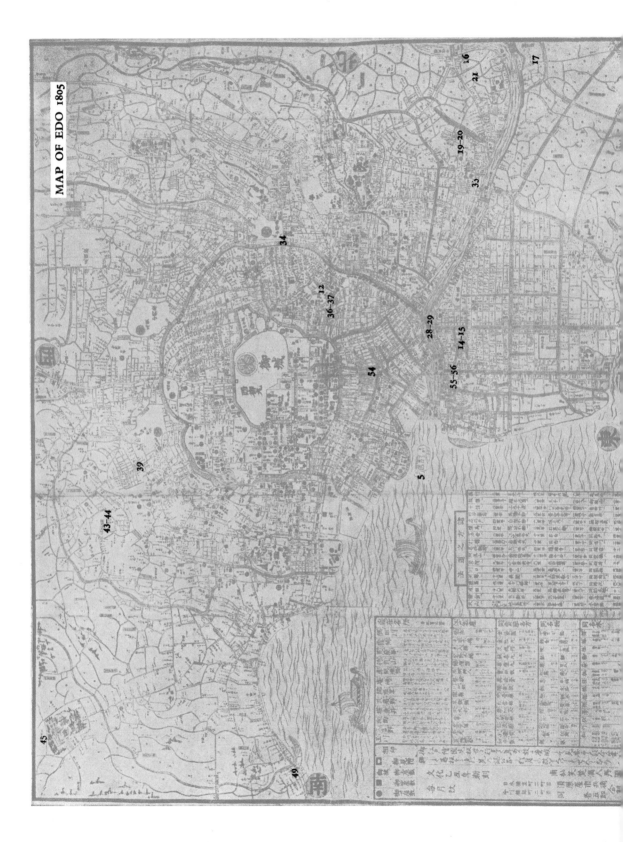

MAP OF EDO 1805

THE PLATES

1. "Umezawa in Sagami Province"

There is some doubt as to the correct title of this print. The title on the print reads, literally, "left of Umezawa," but it is believed that either Hokusai or his printer mistakenly used the Japanese character for "left" in place of another character that would form part of the name of the place. The location would seem to be the present-day Ninomiya, a city near the coast of Kanagawa Prefecture between Kōzu and Odawara. The place affords a classically beautiful view of Mt. Fuji, and the print may have been intended to capture the special atmosphere of the foothills of Mt. Fuji viewed from this vantage point. However, its real artistic value lies elsewhere—in the extraordinary way it suggests the purity and tranquillity of early morning as the dawn of a fine day slowly spreads over the earth. The faintest color tinges the morning mists that still enfold the scene. Most of Mt. Fuji, on the other hand, is still wrapped in shadow, though one senses that at any moment it will be bathed in a pinkish glow. Two cranes flutter off into the brighter air, while five more remain in the shadow on the ground.

2. "In the Mountains of Tōtōmi Province"

This print is famous for its unusual composition, with Mt. Fuji peering out from between two posts supporting a preposterously large piece of timber. Formally speaking, the interest of the print lies in the triangles formed by the wood and the mountain behind, and in the way the smoke from the fire tended by the sturdy country youth in the center of the picture is echoed by the dragon-like clouds writhing about the mountain. The figure of the man plying his saw halfway up the massive timber has often been commented on, but the figure kneeling on the straw mat and attempting to saw the wood from beneath is equally fine. In the figures of the old man setting a saw and the woman carrying a child on her back, one senses the loneliness of the life led by such woodcutters' families, destined to live out their days deep in the hills away from human society. In works such as this, Hokusai leaves the sophisticated town behind and identifies completely with the dwellers in field and forest. He was, by his own choice, a true man of the people.

34

3. "Mishima Pass in the Province of Kai"

A woodcutter sits and enjoys a pipeful of tobacco. Countryfolk who have been working in the mountains disappear along a path down the hillside. A huge cryptomeria tree towers to the heavens at the top of the pass, and a group of travelers stretch their arms about it in an attempt to estimate its girth. Seen from this angle, the summit of Mt. Fuji narrows to a sharp point, and Hokusai embellishes it with a "dragon-type" cloud that looks remarkably like smoke from the crater—although Mt. Fuji had already been dormant for more than a century. The clouds rising on either side of the mountain seem to be imbued with a kind of supernatural life, as though they, too, were living creatures about to engage the dragons at the summit in mortal combat. In such details, one senses the almost mystical awareness of the energies of nature that seems to have inspired the artist in his later years.

4. "Great Wave Off Kanagawa"

Little need be said of a print whose boldness and originality of composition and color are still as much in evidence as ever today, a full century after it first astonished artists in nineteenth-century Europe and America. If the "Red Fuji" shows Hokusai's approach to nature at its most serene and impersonal, this work can be said to demonstrate in extreme form his

awareness of the mighty forces at work within
the natural world, and his sympathy for man
in the face of those forces. Even Mt. Fuji here
is fragile and seemingly about to be engulfed.

5. "The Island of Tsukuda"

One of the projects which engaged the shogunate's attention sporadically from the time of its founding in 1603 was the reclaiming of the sandbanks in the lower reaches of the Sumida River. The island of Tsukuda, the gentle melancholy of whose scenery inspired so many works of art in the Edo period, first came into being in 1644, when the shogun gave an area of reclaimed land about 600 feet square to the fisherfolk of Settsu, and resettled them on it. The sailing vessels in the distance are doubtless lying off the port of Shinagawa, now a railway junction near the heart of modern Tokyo. In this print, the island, with its fishing village and its humble homes buried amidst the trees, has an isolated, almost forlorn air. Today, it is connected with the mainland by a large bridge, and the pure waters of the river estuary are filthy and stinking with the waste of an industrial city. The only time in the past century when the Sumida River came into its own again was in 1945, when the city was largely destroyed and its normal functions were at a standstill.

38

6. "Ushibori in the Province of Hitachi"

Ushibori is a minor port of call for boats on the shore of Kasumi-ga-ura, a large lake which was formerly an inlet of the sea and connects up with the Tone River system in Ibaraki Prefecture. In Hokusai's day, the lake and the marshes about it were a lonely area, but today it is a popular tourist spot. If Hiroshige had depicted this same scene, he would have shown it through the eyes of the visitor from the town, emphasizing or even sentimentalizing its rural charm. Hokusai chooses to make it an opportunity for a realistic portrayal of the lonely life of a family living its life out on a barge. The complete unsentimentality with which he treats the subject suggests concern for humanity that the more facile Hiroshige never felt. Two snowy herons fly off over the rushes, disturbed by the man washing rice.

7–8. "Kajikazawa in the Province of Kai"

Kajikazawa is a picturesque spot on the River Fuji, which gathers together the waters of the streams rushing down from the many-tiered mountains of Kai and pours them into the ocean at Suruga Bay. In the scene shown here, heavy rain must have fallen recently. One seems almost to hear the roar of the river as it rushes swollen down to the sea, dashing itself against its banks and its beds of rocks, its waves clawing wildly at the sky. An old fisherman stands on a spur of land jutting out over the water, holding his lines in his hand, while a boy crouches over the basket in which the fish are kept. A faint sun seems to be breaking through the mist and cloud, brightening the green of the bank. The triangle formed by the fisherman with his lines and the spur of land on which he stands echoes the triangle of Mt. Fuji. The human element, and the quiet sympathy that Hokusai shows for those who eke out a living in the remote country districts are surely as impressive as the composition.

9. "Eijiri in the Province of Suruga"

Hokusai's idea in this print was borrowed by Hiroshige for a work in his "Fifty-three Stations on the Tōkaidō" which shows a traveler whose hat has been blown away by the autumn breeze. In Hokusai's work, a strong gust of wind has made off with leaves from the tree, one of the traveler's hats, and even the sheets of tissue paper which the woman—as everybody did at the time—was carrying tucked in the breast of her kimono. As they whirl up into the air, they make a fine, amusing sight for anyone not directly involved. The work particularly illustrates Hokusai's consummate skill with human figures. It is strange that he should not have taken more trouble with the composition of Mt. Fuji and its foothills. The use of brown for the sky, with its suggestion of bad weather in the offing, is especially effective.

10 and *(overleaf)* 11. "Minobu River"

Hokusai once wrote that if he lived to be over a hundred his art would become like life itself, and in this print one feels, indeed, that a mysterious vitality is already stirring within his forms—in the horses that, if one gazes at them for a while, seem almost to be moving across the paper; in the water of the river, with its stylized suggestion of the rocky bed below; in the trees at right center; in the craggy, fantastic mountains; and in the peak of Mt. Fuji thrusting up between them. Hokusai's studies of old brush paintings in his younger days must have included the colored landscapes of Ming and Ching dynasties, for he has succeeded here in translating their richness and brilliance into terms of the woodblock print.

12. "Surugadai in Edo"

The area of land rising above the banks of the Kanda River in what is now the Ochanomizu district of Tokyo was noted for its distant view of Mt. Fuji, and frequently appeared in pictures. Part of the river still survives today, and riding in a crowded train one may yet catch sight of a dredging boat drifting beneath willow trees in a scene that could have been duplicated in old Edo. In this print, a variety of figures— a samurai with his attendants, a traveler, a pilgrim, a merchant—are passing up or down a sunny slope on a hot summer's day. On the right, part of an imposing samurai residence is visible, and in the center foreground part of a wayside stall. All around is the luxuriant summer foliage of trees, their uppermost branches stretching up into the azure of the sky. Mt. Fuji, with its northern slope hidden and the snow melting on its southern slope, is enveloped in an amber haze. The use of a combination of blue, yellow, blue-green and yellow-green, which so skillfully suggests the strong summer sunlight, must have required considerable skill on the part of the printer.

46

13. "Hodogaya on the Tōkaidō"

Rows of pine trees such as these, their branches linked against the azure of the sky, were once a familiar sight on the Tōkaidō highway, but the old highway has been replaced by modern motor roads, and the pines themselves have almost all disappeared. In Hokusai's day, Hodogaya was a country spot near the coast, and the graceful form of Mt. Fuji would be the traveler's constant companion, now on his left, now on his right, as he made his way along the winding road. Today, Hodogaya is a heavily built-up district of Yokohama, the last stop before Yokohama for all the local trains bound for Tokyo. The bare-headed groom seems to be smitten with the view of Mt. Fuji, but the figure on horseback bows his head beneath his large traveler's hat, doubtless lost in memories of the thriving city of Edo that he has left behind, or of the cities of Kyoto and Osaka to which the road will eventually lead. The snows on the southern slopes of the mountain are already melting, a sign that the season is late spring. The curved line in the lower half of the picture, dividing the foreground from the middle distance, was a compositional device that Hiroshige often imitated.

14–15. "Honjo Tatekawa, Edo"

This print relies on the beauty of straight lines for much of its effect. The poles in the timber-yard on the right reaching straight up into the sky, intersect the slopes of Mt. Fuji and the horizontal layer of haze; the heavy timbers and the lengths of green bamboo in the foreground are balanced by the piece of wood which a workman is busily sawing; and the great square piles of firewood on the left are counter-weighted by the pattern of roofs that lies to their right—a series of complex geometrical patterns that add up to a very beautiful work. A touch of light relief is provided by the figures of two workmen on the left, one of whom is throwing a piece of wood up to the other. An inscription on a piece of timber on the right suggests that this print was the first of the ten supplementary works to the series.

16. "Senjū in the Province of Musashi"

The place known as Senjū—today well within the confines of metropolitan Tokyo—was most important in Hokusai's day. The Senjū Bridge across the Senjū River (a branch of what is collectively known as the Sumida River) was the starting point of the Ōshū Highway, one of the main highways leading out of Edo to the provinces, and the point from which all distances along the highway were measured. There were naturally many inns near the bridge, and the district was already a busy one, but Hokusai chose to turn his back on human habitation and gaze over the floodgate and across a typical scene of paddy fields and open country, to where Mt. Fuji trailed its long slopes in the distance. Another artist might have been more perfunctory in his treatment of the anglers on the left of the picture, but Hokusai succeeds wonderfully in conveying their postures and their absorption in their pastime. He even adds a touch of humor, in the way the horse is so obviously chafing with impatience.

17. "Sekiya-no-sato on the Sumida River"

Nowadays, Sekiya-no-sato is a bustling district in Senjū in Adachi Ward, Tokyo, but in Hokusai's time this same spot on the Sumida River was a lonely stretch of country which travelers, having forded the river, had to cross on their way from Edo to the Chiba peninsula or the northeastern districts of Honshu. It was a favorite haunt of artists and men of letters, who went there in search of rustic solitude and were moved to a gentle melancholy by the sight of wild geese settling on the harvested paddy fields. In this print, the rice still stands unharvested in the fields, and three samurai on horseback are shown galloping off in the direction of Edo along the winding path between the paddies. One seems almost to hear the thudding of hooves and the neighing of horses as they disappear into the distance across the wide spaces of the Musashino plain. The composition directs the eye along the raised embankment from the foreground in the direction the riders are taking, and the effect of distant, red Mt. Fuji as it comes into one's field of vision on the right is particularly striking.

18. "Red Fuji"
This print, along with the "Great Wave Off Kanagawa," is one of Hokusai's two most famous works. The extraordinary simplicity of the subject matter, the boldness of the composition with its subtle feeling for proportions, and

the freshness and originality of the coloring,
all came as a revelation to art circles in the
West when Hokusai's work first became
known there in the nineteenth century.

19–20. "Ōno Shinden in the Province of Suruga"

This print exhibits a remarkably skillful combination of a remotely ethereal, rather stylized background and an almost grotesquely down-to-earth foreground. Ōno Shinden is in present-day Yoshiwara city, but in this work nothing but a stretch of misty marshland separates the viewer from Mt. Fuji, which is shown in one of its most graceful aspects. Another mountain, Mt. Ashitaka shows dark and forbidding on the right beyond Mt. Fuji's snow-covered slopes. The graceful effect of the background is heightened by the five snowy herons seen flying away into the distance. The foreground forms a startling contrast. Along the road passes a group of peasants leading oxen carrying loads of dark-colored rushes. The scene is homely in the extreme, yet the two parts of the print harmonize perfectly.

21. "The Gay Quarters at Senjū"

In the foreground, a daimyo's procession is passing. Two samurai are seen on the extreme right, followed by a single file of musket-bearers and, behind them again, more men carrying lances, which are visible above the thatched roof on the left. Doubtless they are on their way back to their homes in the country after a spell in Edo with their lord, who would have been obliged by official shogunate policy to spend half of every year in Edo. In the background, within their high surrounding fence, the gay quarters lie still and somnolent beneath the daytime sun. The two peasant women sitting on the raised path between the fields seem to be talking to each other about the procession. The palanquin-bearer who is looking into the resthouse on the right is wearing a jacket bearing the mark of the print's publisher, Eijudō. But only the last man visible in the procession, shading his eyes with his hand, seems to be concerned with the gradually disappearing view of Mt. Fuji.

22. "Tea Garden at Katakura in Suruga Province"

A row of women wearing round sedge hats are busily picking tea, while others are resting on a long bench nearby. A similar scene is visible in the field beyond, the positions of the two groups being reversed with an effectiveness typical of Hokusai's eye for variation. The large amount of detail in the foreground, where men and horses are seen going about the business of the tea garden, suggests that this print was intended primarily as a genre picture. Mt. Fuji here seems to be rather irrelevant to the print as a whole, and the composition is not so interesting as in some other works in the series, but there is much to compensate for this in the interest and clarity of the detail, even in the more distant parts of the scene.

23. "The Bay at Tago"

Mention of Tago Bay at once calls to the mind of any Japanese the celebrated poem in the *Manyōshū* anthology which tells how the poet went out in a boat from Tago Bay and was overcome by the view of the snow-covered mountain that suddenly came into his sight. Possibly Hokusai was inspired by the same poem when he made this print. The most impressive feature of the work is not the boats being rowed out from the bay, nor even the long, gracefully curving line of the first boat, but the extraordinary care the artist has taken over the scene on the shore, with its mat-covered shacks, the figures collecting sea water for making salt, and other figures raking in salt from the dried beds.

24 and *(overleaf)* 25. "Kanaya on the Tōkaidō"

The scene is the ford between Kanaya, the village visible on the opposite bank of the river, and Shimada, on the near bank. On the left, an enormous piece of baggage rides the waves proudly, borne on the shoulders of a band of at least twenty men. Coming to meet it from the opposite bank are two more groups, carrying a palanquin and another bundle respectively. Another group bearing a palanquin waits in the rear, stooping slightly beneath the weight. In the foreground, travelers are being carried across the river on porters' backs. The exaggerated stylization of the waves, which form a series of blue and white bands against which the figures create patterns of color, achieves a broadly decorative effect of great beauty. Hokusai's customary attention to detail and his feeling for the human figure are evident in the near-naked porters seen soliciting customers or simply resting on the far bank.

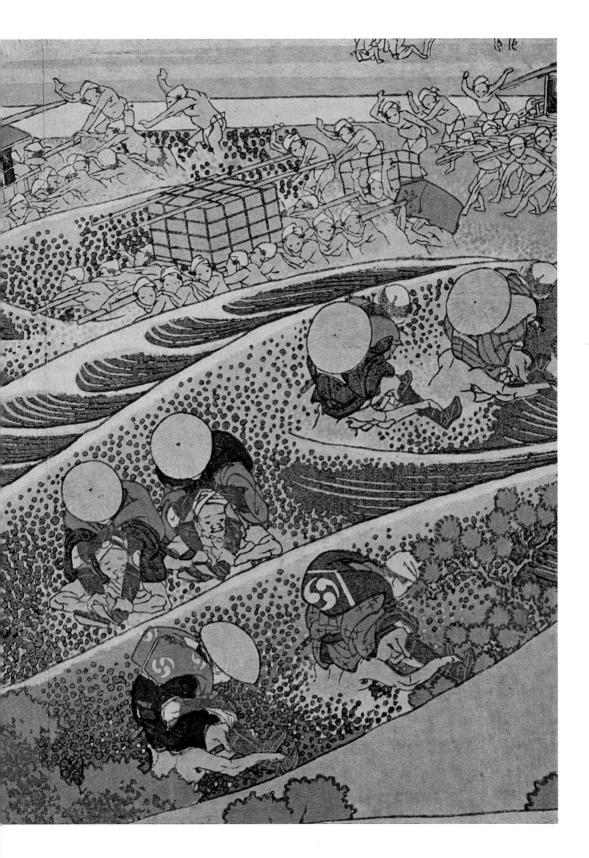

26. "Enoshima in the Province of Sagami"

This print, for a Hokusai landscape, is extra-ordinarily faithful to reality, though Mt. Fuji should in fact lie somewhat farther to the left. Enoshima lies just off the shore, not far from Kamakura and only ninety minutes or so from modern Tokyo. Not long ago, one still reached it at low tide by walking along the exposed sand, avoiding remaining pools as one went, but today a modern concrete bridge connects it to the mainland. The tiny figures crossing to the island in this scene are all, when seen more closely, astonishingly alive.

27. "Nakahara in the Province of Sagami"

A typical peasant woman is seen crossing the bridge. A child is on her back, she carries a hoe in her right hand, carefully balanced at one end with an iron kettle, and with her left hand supports a round tray containing a meal to be eaten in the fields. Every detail is right, down to the way she places her feet as she walks. The man on her right is a peddler with his wares suspended from a pole on his shoulder. The scene is a country road at a spot which is now within the city of Hiratsuka, and the religious ascetic (second from the right) is doubtless on his way to the sacred mountain of Ōyama which lies nearby. The man on the left is catching fish in the river, while the man with his belongings on his back who is about to cross the bridge is obviously young, and good-looking in the fashion of the day. In short, this is a typical scene on a much-frequented country road in Hokusai's day, and the interest of its detail compensates for the lack of interest in the composition.

28–29. "Sunset Over Ryōgoku Bridge, Seen From Oumaya Pier"

The boat rocks gently; the setting sun has finally disappeared beyond the western bank of the river; the ruddy glow has receded from the clouds; and the inky-black curtain of night begins to fall over the city. In the deep-blue cone of Mt. Fuji, silhouetted against the last light of the day, Hokusai has given a focus to his whole picture. He links together the sky and the scene below by his skillful placing of the rod which the man in the boat, on his way home from a day's fishing, holds upright in his hand. The dark curve of Ryōgoku Bridge, green-tinged in the evening light, is echoed in reverse by the curve of the ferryboat rocking on the river's swell, and the same motif is taken up and repeated in the waves rolling against the bank. A similar repetition of motif can be seen in the circles formed by the umbrella, the straw hats, and the ferryman's bald pate. Even more than the composition, it is the coloring —the combinations of black, indigo, and green —that account for the success of this work which has always been considered one of the masterpieces of the series.

64

65

30. "Lake Suwa in the Province of Shinano"
Today, this area is a center of the precision-machinery industry, and a series of large factories have changed its appearance completely. In the foreground of the print stands a typical small country shrine, with two aged pine trees growing by its side. In the distance, on the left, stands Takashima castle. The boat on the lake is probably fishing for smelt, for which the lake is famous. Otherwise, no sign of life disturbs the tranquillity of the scene.

31. "Shichirigahama in the Province of Sagami"

Hiroshige and others were later to produce many more pictures of this same spot, which lies on the coast near Kamakura. However, their works all aim at a kind of picture-postcard literalness, whereas Hokusai's print is a pure exercise in landscape for its own sake, with little save the title to indicate where the scene is supposed to be. The clouds shown rising in the golden-brown, distant sky are a feature which first put in its appearance in Hokusai's Western-style pictures, and are possibly derived from Western painting.

32. "Tamagawa River in the Province of Musashi"

The Tamagawa flows into the ocean in the heavily industrialized area between Tokyo and Yokohama, but until recently one had only to go a little way upstream, to the outskirts of the city, to find open country left much as Hokusai and Hiroshige must have known it. Now, apparently, there are plans to build estates of multi-story apartment buildings on the river's banks, which will be traversed on both sides by modern expressways. Soon, the sight of the moon rising over the rushes bordering the river, will be a thing of the past.

33. "The Hongan-ji Temple at Asakusa in Edo"

Hokusai's main purpose in this print was probably to contrast the flimsy scaffolding erected high above the close ranks of tiled roofs on the left, and the massive solidity of the roof of the Hongan-ji Temple on the right. The detail with which the ridge tiles, the gable, and the bracket systems beneath are treated, automatically draws one's eye to the right of the picture, and it is only then that one notices the five workmen who, with comical exaggeration, are completely dwarfed by the great roof which they are repairing. The deliberate echoing of the triangular shape of the mountain in the triangle of the gable probably represents an attempt to give the picture spatial depth. The unusual concept and composition rather than any atmospheric, emotional effect gives the print its chief interest.

34. "Snowy Morning in Koishikawa"

Koishikawa is located in what is now Bunkyo Ward, Tokyo, but there is no indication of the exact spot represented here. Wherever it is, one would need a telescopic lens for Mt. Fuji to appear as close as it is shown in this print. That the mountain— albeit somewhat smaller —was in fact visible from various parts of the city is witnessed by the frequent occurrence of the word *Fujimi* ("Fuji View") in contemporary place-names. For some reason Hokusai, unlike Hiroshige, was not attracted by snowy scenes, and this is one of his very few snowscapes. A party of men and women is shown drinking saké and enjoying the view. One of the women points up at the sky, where three birds are flying.

35. "Fujimihara in the Province of Owari"

In this print, Mt. Fuji, framed in the ring formed by an enormous wooden tub in the making, rises distant and snow-covered beyond a stretch of dried-up paddy fields where the earth has cracked in almost geometrical patterns. Green bamboo for use in making the hoops of the tub lies on the ground nearby, forming two more circles and demonstrating in very simple yet striking form the fondness for a composition of triangular and circular elements that shows itself so often in Hokusai's work. The old workman busy inside the tub is depicted with consummate skill, and the print is deservedly one of the most celebrated in the whole series. Whether or not there was a real place called Fujimihara in Owari is not clear. However, this is obviously a scene in the remote countryside, and it might not be too fanciful to see in the yellow of the bank on the left a suggestion of the rape blossom that abounds in such areas in spring and early summer.

36–37. "The Mitsui Store at Suruga-machi in Edo"

The sign on the right says, in large letters, "Dry Goods," and, in smaller letters above, "Cash Payment, Fixed Prices." Contemporary pictures of other famous stores such as Echigo-ya and Shiroki-ya invariably show similar signs, which tell us something about the type of economy that had developed in Edo by this time. This print is a typical example of Hokusai's interest in the compositional possibilities of tall buildings and the three-dimensional, geometrical effects they could produce. The perspective, as often happens in Hokusai's work, is exceedingly unnatural, but one suspects that such considerations for Hokusai were secondary to his desire to capture the scene as one of the workmen, perched precariously on the slope of the roof, stretches out to catch the bundle of tiles flung up to him.

38. "The Bay at Noboto"

In his youth, Hokusai produced another picture of the same bay in which he employed techniques from Western painting and signed his name horizontally in imitation of foreign script. Artistically, this print is inferior to the earlier work. The central subject is the two *torii,* gateways to the Noboto shrine, part of the roof of which can be seen in the lower right-hand corner. Somehow, they do not seem to fit into the composition very well. Whatever one's opinion of the print as a whole, however, the treatment of the local folk shown collecting shellfish at low tide is remarkable. The delicacy with which Hokusai captures the movements of limbs and muscles, gestures, and even shades of facial expression, is astonishing even to someone already familiar with his work.

39. "The 'Round Cushion' Pine at Aoyama"

In the grounds of the Ryōgan-ji temple in Aoyama, not far from the heart of modern Tokyo, there used to stand a magnificent pine tree—popularly known as the "round cushion" pine—whose many branches spread out over a large area of the garden. It was a popular pastime among the citizens of Edo to repair to the temple and exchange cups of saké as they savored the contrast between the pointed peak of Mt. Fuji, rising above the distant mists, and the verdant cone formed by the nearby tree. A typically humorous touch is provided in this print by the single leg of a temple employe—obviously at work pruning the tree,—which is visible beneath the low-hanging branches on the left of the picture.

75

40. "Thunderstorm Below the Mountain"
The lower flanks of the mountain are buried in dark clouds,
lightning forks menacingly, the valleys beneath are shaken
by peals of thunder, and man, unseen below, cowers before
the might of nature. Yet at the mountain's summit the sky

is serene, with curly white clouds in the distance and the peaks of the Southern Alps rising majestic against a cerulean backdrop. The startling contrast of light and shadow, and the use of shading all add to the effect of this work, which, with the "Red Fuji" and the "Great Wave Off Kanagawa," is one of the three most famous prints in the series.

41. "Dawn at Isawa in the Province of Kai"
Isawa on the River Fuefuki—in Hokusai's time the final stage on the highway leading to the important town of Kōfu—was unremarkable for anything save its fireflies until, some years ago, the discovery of an excellent hot spring touched off a gradual transformation. On one of his trips to the provinces, Hokusai spent some time in and around Kōfu, and pictures survive that he did at the time. In this print, he shows travelers about to set off in the pre-dawn half-light, with the damp air from the river striking chill on their cheeks. The mist lies thick and heavy, but above it Mt. Fuji is visible, towering dark against the sky's first flush of dawn. In reality, other mountains obscure the view of Mt. Fuji from Isawa, and one would have to climb very high to see its lower slopes as they are shown here.

42. "Climbing the Mountain"

Clouds are rising and filling the valleys, invisible from a distance, that scar Mt. Fuji's flanks. The chanting of pilgrims is heard, and men are seen clambering up the zigzag route to the summit, aided by the staffs they all carry and even, it seems, by ladders when necessary. Some of them, wearied by the climb, are gathered in a cave where they crouch down close together, possibly because of the cold. The contours of the bare volcanic rock carry a vivid suggestion of the living, moving, substance that it was until only recently. Trees at this height are, of course, no more than a piece of artistic license. The ascent today, with buses up to the fifth station, is less arduous, and women are no longer barred from the mountain, but the summit is still no more prepossessing, seen at close quarters, than this picture suggests.

43–44. "The Waterwheel at Onden"

The Onden area is now traversed by a broad, modern avenue running from the main Aoyama street to the Meiji Shrine in Tokyo. Few things bring home more vividly a sense of the changing times than a comparison of this print with the district as it is today, with its modern apartment houses and its unceasing flow of traffic. In the days when Hokusai and Hiroshige strolled through it with their sketching materials, the area was still largely rural, relying partly on commerce and partly on agriculture. Its houses were scattered, and streams still flowed through its gently undulating fields. To the sophisticated town-dweller of the day, the presence of such a waterwheel would have been a great attraction, and its gentle creaking a source of solace to the mind weary of worldly affairs. What attracted Hokusai, however, was the movement of the water as it fell from the wheel and flowed away along its conduit.

45. "Lower Meguro"

Japan is famous for the way its hillsides are cultivated in terraces wherever this is humanly possible. A good example is seen in this print; it is interesting how Hokusai uses the pattern created by the terraces for a curiously modern effect in the composition of the hills on the right. The area shown may well be that part of Meguro where there was a resthouse called "Fuji View" in Hokusai's time. Whatever the case, Hokusai is not concerned with such things here, but sets out to show a typical rural scene in what was then the outskirts of Edo, giving the print a kind of focus in the figure of a peasant who stands on the left, half turning round as though to gaze back to where Mt. Fuji is visible in a gap in the hills.

46. "The Lake at Hakone in Sagami Province" This is scarcely one of the most impressive works in the series. Even so, there is a freshness and purity about the scene that rescues it from mere dullness, and a skillful suggestion of the stillness of deep waters amidst lofty mountains. In a picture of the same lake by Hiroshige, the stillness has an emotional, atmospheric effect, but here the impact is purely visual; the stillness is cold, like the cold surface of the lake's waters. Possibly Hokusai's rather feeble reliance on stereotype "glove clouds" of the kind in use ever since the earliest days of the *Yamato-e* carries with it a suggestion of graphic design that somehow alienates the emotions.

47. "Inume Pass in the Province of Kai"
Inume Pass is still a remote spot in the mountains, and the view remains very much as Hokusai has shown it here. Of all the prints in the series, this uses the most complicated color scheme for Mt. Fuji itself, and the subtle shades are effectively

interposed between the white of the cloud that hangs about its lower slopes and the clear amber of the sky above. The two figures clambering up the pathless hillside are clearly travelers, while the two figures below, talking to each other as their packhorses trudge silently in their wake, are local inhabitants on their way from one village to another.

48. "The Sazaidō of the Gohyaku Rakan-ji Temple"

This temple was an imposing complex of buildings in Hokusai's time. One of them, the Sazaidō, was a three-story structure that afforded an excellent view of Mt. Fuji. The man of the merchant class who leans against the railing with his kimono sleeves rolled up, the woman beside him who looks like his wife, and the young apprentice with arm outstretched, are all looking towards the mountain, so that one's gaze is led naturally in the same direction. The eye is drawn back to the foreground by the two figures on the right, a man and wife on a religious pilgrimage who have just set their bundles down on the floor for a well-earned rest. The details of the eaves and the brackets beneath them, and the lines of the boards are all drawn with great precision, everything seeming to enhance the sense of movement and direction—with Mt. Fuji itself the point at which everything converges.

49. "Goten-yama at Shinagawa on the
Tōkaidō Highway"

Shinagawa, overlooking the sea, afforded a wider prospect than other famous cherry-viewing spots in Edo, and was a favorite among the inhabitants of the city in the spring. In this work, a number of them are seen enjoying themselves on a fine spring day with the trees in full bloom. The numerous elements within the composition are handled with extraordinary skill. The low hills in the center of the print form a winding line, while the human figures form another, longer winding line which is the mainstay of the composition. Starting with the group of figures enjoying their saké in style on the left, it passes through the man and wife carrying children on their backs, on through the tipsy, rather disreputable-looking group in front of the small building, and ends with the travelers shown disappearing into the distance—though it seems to point on still further, to the graceful form of Mt. Fuji seen rising above the distant hills. Perhaps the finest individual section of the print is the left-hand corner, with the roofs forming a pattern against the blue sea, the figures on their mat, and the interspersed greenery of the trees.

88

50–51. "Yoshida on the Tōkaidō"

This print shows a scene in a teahouse at Yoshida, now part of the modern city of Toyohashi, in Aichi Prefecture. In the center, visible below the short, dark-blue, divided curtain that once hung at the entrance of all shops and restaurants, a large sign proclaims the "Fuji View Teahouse," a common name for such establishments. Two women travelers have alighted from their palanquins (one of which is visible on the extreme left), and are taking their ease while a waitress points out the view of Mt. Fuji for them. The delicate contrast and balance of the two women's poses is a reminder that Hokusai was also a master of the "beautiful woman" picture. The characters on the hat and clothes of the man who slumps, tired out, at the right of the print form the name of the publisher. While everybody else rests, the odd-jobman of the teahouse is still hard at work repairing a pair of straw sandals, and Hokusai seems almost to be evoking sympathy for his pitifully emaciated body.

52. "At Sea Off Kazusa"

The ships are blessed with perfect weather. Wherever one looks, the sky stretches blue and cloudless over a sea with only the smallest waves crinkling its surface like crepe. The arc formed by the ship in the foreground is effectively countered by the long, gentle curve of the horizon where sea and sky meet, the effect being heightened by the shading of the sea from deep blue in the foreground to pale green just below the horizon. The small white form of Mt. Fuji provides an admirable focus of interest, and the yellow of the bare hills reflecting the sun on the extreme right is a vivid touch of light and life. The inhabitants of Edo had not long before been astonished by reports, brought by the Dutch, that the earth was spherical, and Hokusai may have been displaying his knowledge in this print.

53. "The Lake at Misaka in the Province
of Kai"

Mt. Fuji is reflected in the still, mirror-like waters of the lake, but why the real mountain should be shown unusually craggy and apparently bare of snow, whereas its reflection shows the more familiar form capped with snow, remains a mystery. It is all the more strange in that Hokusai was not given to such irrationalities in his work. Whatever the explanation, the print is a landscape masterpiece. Lake, hills, trees, and even human habitations are sunk in a profound stillness, standing out clear and bright in the mist-free, pellucid atmosphere. The only sign of life is the solitary fisherman in his boat, whose presence seems only to heighten the pervading serenity.

54. "Nihonbashi Bridge in Edo"
The "Thirty-six Views" were conceived with Edo as a kind of
focal point, and the focal point of Edo in its turn was the Nihonbashi Bridge. In this print Hokusai, with his characteristic skill
in depicting the human scene, reduces the bridge to a bustling

melee of heads, arms, hats, bundles, bales, and even baskets of food. The perspective, with the foreground rapidly narrowing to a point in the center of the print and a T-shaped background lying beyond it, is of a kind commonly found in the *uki-e*, a type of picture which used an exaggerated Western-style perspective and was popular around the same period.

55-56. "Mannenbashi Bridge at Fukagawa"

The Mannenbashi Bridge at Fukagawa in Edo crossed a smaller river just at the point where it flowed into the great Sumida River. Hokusai exaggerates the height of the piers, creating an effect as though one were gazing up at the bridge from a boat on the water, and sets the distant Mt. Fuji between them, with the buildings on the opposite bank of the larger river at its foot. The resulting perspective is rather disturbing, but Hokusai's concern here was obviously not a strictly rational perspective, but an interesting composition based on his favorite circle-and-triangle theme. A noteworthy feature of this print is the use of Western-style chiaroscuro on the trees on either side of the picture. Town residences of feudal lords, rice warehouses, and other buildings line the bank.

94

57. Detail to "Mishima Pass in the Province
of Kai" (Plate 3)

96